HAZMAT
DISPOSING TOXIC MATERIALS

Emma Carlson Berne

Rourke
Educational Media
rourkeeducationalmedia.com

Scan for Related Titles and
Teacher Resources

Before Reading:

Building Academic Vocabulary and Background Knowledge

Before reading a book, it is important to tap into what your child or students already know about the topic. This will help them develop their vocabulary, increase their reading comprehension, and make connections across the curriculum.

1. *Look at the cover of the book. What will this book be about?*
2. *What do you already know about the topic?*
3. *Let's study the Table of Contents. What will you learn about in the book's chapters?*
4. *What would you like to learn about this topic? Do you think you might learn about it from this book? Why or why not?*
5. *Use a reading journal to write about your knowledge of this topic. Record what you already know about the topic and what you hope to learn about the topic.*
6. *Read the book.*
7. *In your reading journal, record what you learned about the topic and your response to the book.*
8. *After reading the book complete the activities below.*

Content Area Vocabulary

Read the list. What do these words mean?

anthrax
deputies
evacuation
evaluate
hazardous
methamphetamine
neutralize
substances
terrorism

After Reading:

Comprehension and Extension Activity

After reading the book, work on the following questions with your child or students in order to check thei level of reading comprehension and content mastery.

1. *Name some symbols that represent hazardous materials. (Summarize)*
2. *In what situations might hazardous materials explode or catch fire? (Infer)*
3. *If you were ever a witness to a spilled, hazardous material what should you do? (Text to self connectio*
4. *What does the word HAZMAT stand for? (Asking Questions)*
5. *What is the most important piece of gear for a hazmat worker? (Asking Questions)*

Extension Activity

Suppose you are interested in being a member of a hazmat team. Gather reading materials on what type of training you would need to receive in order to obtain this position. With the help of an adult, research websites on what types of things you would have to do on a daily basis. Fold a sheet of paper in half and label one side ADVANTAGES. On the other side, label with DISADVANTAGES. See whether this job is rig for you by comparing how many reasons for or against you have on both sides of your paper.

TABLE OF CONTENTS

Community Clean-Up 4

Who Is the Hazmat Team? 8

Helping to Keep Citizens Safe 12

All Geared Up 17

Protecting Against Terrorism 24

Timeline 28

Glossary 30

Index 31

Show What You Know 31

Websites to Visit... 31

About the Author 32

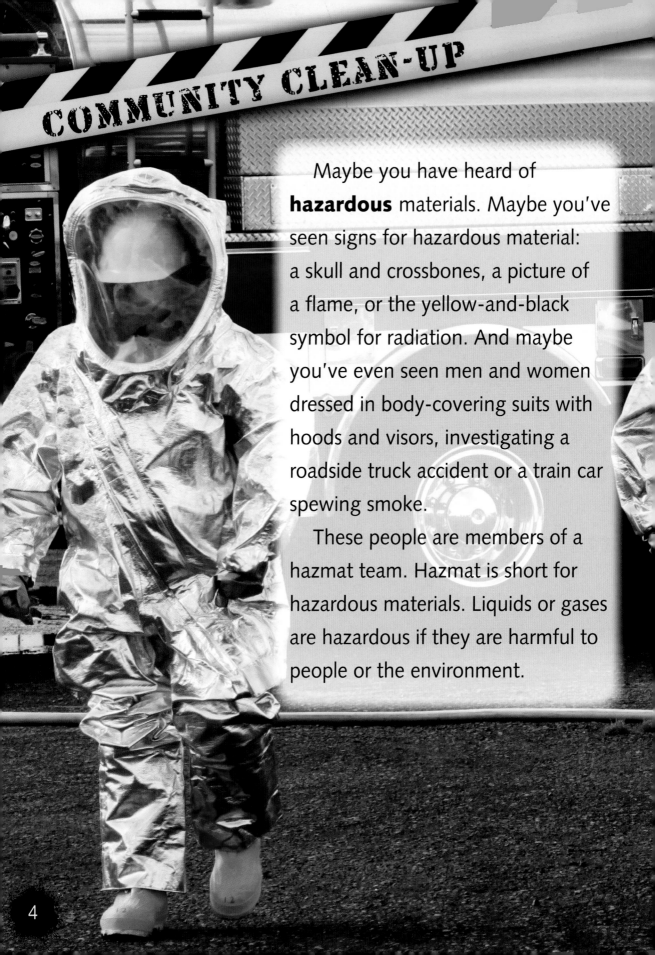

Maybe you have heard of **hazardous** materials. Maybe you've seen signs for hazardous material: a skull and crossbones, a picture of a flame, or the yellow-and-black symbol for radiation. And maybe you've even seen men and women dressed in body-covering suits with hoods and visors, investigating a roadside truck accident or a train car spewing smoke.

These people are members of a hazmat team. Hazmat is short for hazardous materials. Liquids or gases are hazardous if they are harmful to people or the environment.

EMERGENCY FACT
Hazmat teams sometimes help clean up chemicals that are so strong, they can dissolve human flesh.

When trucks, trains or ships carrying hazardous materials have accidents, the liquids or gases inside may leak, catch fire, or explode. Sometimes plants or factories that use these materials have accidents. The dangerous **substances** can escape. Hazmat teams have special training on how to safely contain and clean up these spills, so that no one else is harmed.

36 IN IW STEEL WHEELS
SPRING D-3   MCVX 40345
25367 GALS
89765 LITERS

MCVX 4034

LD LMT   176000 85200 KGS
LT WT   87000 44000 KGS

Spill Response Team
00 33.SPILL

A913992

Hazmat drills are an opportunity for team growth in that it builds confidence, and prepares the members of the team for future disasters.

Hazmat teams are usually a part of a sheriff's office or a fire department. Sometimes, they are connected to a university. The team members respond to any incident day or night, just like firefighters. In fact, many hazmat team members are firefighters. Some are sheriff's **deputies**. Others are volunteers from the community.

Hazmat team members attend more than one hundred and fifty hours of training. They learn how to deal with dangerous chemicals in dangerous situations. They are taught how to manage their equipment and work together as a team. Every year, hazmat workers go to more classes to learn about new techniques and new chemicals.

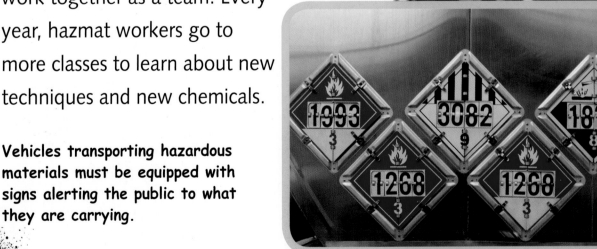

Vehicles transporting hazardous materials must be equipped with signs alerting the public to what they are carrying.

Firefighters, working alongside a hazmat team, work to safely clean up a propane leak.

Counties or fire departments first formed many hazmat teams in the 1970s and 1980s. Officials realized that the chemicals traveling by train or truck through their communities could be quite dangerous. Community leaders asked their local firefighters to volunteer for training in how to manage spills. Thanks to this training, hazmat teams are able to respond quickly to disasters like dangerous chemical spills.

In 2010, the protective lining of a tanker carrying nitric acid failed. The truck's driver pulled off the road and called for help. The driver got out of the truck and the acid started pouring out. The hazmat team arrived on the scene and moved the driver to a safe place. They waited for the truck to stop draining. Then they neutralized the acid and vacuumed it up into another truck whose protective lining was working.

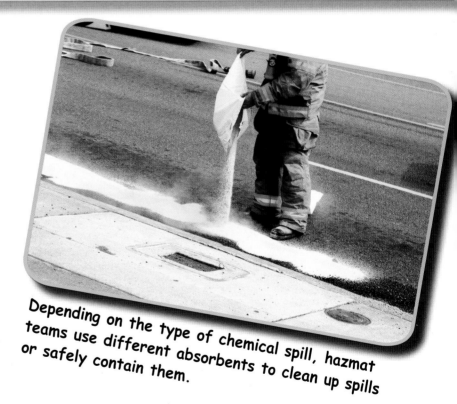

Depending on the type of chemical spill, hazmat teams use different absorbents to clean up spills or safely contain them.

Hazmat workers in full body covering suits work alongside a firefighter in a simulated spill for training purposes.

Usually, the fire department is first to respond to calls about accidents involving dangerous chemicals. The firefighters will put out any fires and move people to safety. Then, they will call in the hazmat team. When the team arrives on the scene, they first **evaluate** the situation. Is the chemical in danger of exploding? Will people nearby be harmed by breathing fumes?

A hazmat team is called in to work with firefighters to evaluate a chemical spill and determine the best course of action to protect people and the environment.

Some hazmat teams have a mobile weather station on their trucks. They monitor the weather to know if the wind will carry a dangerous gas over a town or neighborhood. If it is possible that more people will come into danger, hazmat teams will organize an **evacuation**. If they suspect that someone has released a hazardous substance on purpose, they will call in the police and FBI.

An Oil Spill Response Team was called in after Superstorm Sandy hit the East Coast of the United States.

EMERGENCY FACT

The Jacksonville, Florida hazmat team is busy. They go on 700 to 800 hazardous material calls a year. That's more than two calls every day.

In July 1986, a train carrying an explosive chemical called yellow phosphorus went off its rails in Ohio. The latch holding the tank closed was damaged, and the chemical spilled.

To make matters worse, the train was carrying sulfur, which can form an extremely toxic gas when mixed with yellow phosphorus.

The city officials, the hazmat teams, and the police and fire departments decided to evacuate the area. After looking at all their options, the hazmat teams decided to let the phosphorus burn itself out. They managed the fire, carefully, keeping the flames under control with water.

Hazmat Teams Battle Meth Labs

People manufacture the illegal drug **methamphetamine** using a variety of chemicals, tubes, and bottles. All together, this set-up is called a meth lab. The chemicals that remain in the lab after the methamphetamine is taken out can be explosive. Hazmat teams are often called out to investigate abandoned meth labs. They evaluate the chemicals inside and carefully defuse the labs.

Level B suits are not airtight, so they provide protection against solids and liquids, but not gasses.

Level A suits are total containment suits, giving protection from all forms of chemicals: solids, liquids, and gasses.

The most important piece of gear for any hazmat worker is a protective suit that covers the entire body. These suits are made of a thick plastic that chemicals cannot get through. There are two kinds of hazmat suits. Level B suits protect the wearer from dangerous liquids. While Level A suits offer a wider protection from gases, vapors, and liquids.

Traditional hazmat suits don't offer protection from all dangers. If there is risk of a fire or explosion, hazmat team members must add a flash suit over their hazmat suit.

Hazmat workers also wear a hood with a visor. They wear thick gloves and boots. The hood, gloves, and boots are all taped to the suit, so no splashes or gases can get in.

Team members wear respirators or oxygen tanks so they have safe air to breathe. They use a radio to communicate with others. They even carry a knife, in case they have to quickly get out of their suits in an emergency.

A hazmat worker in full body covering with visor bears grueling temperatures to complete a mission.

Hazmat suits can get very hot: twenty to thirty degrees above the outside air temperature. Team members sometimes wear cooling packs near their skin so they don't overheat.

If a hazmat team member is wearing all the protection available, he or she may be wearing five layers of gloves, five layers of foot protection, and three layers of face visors!

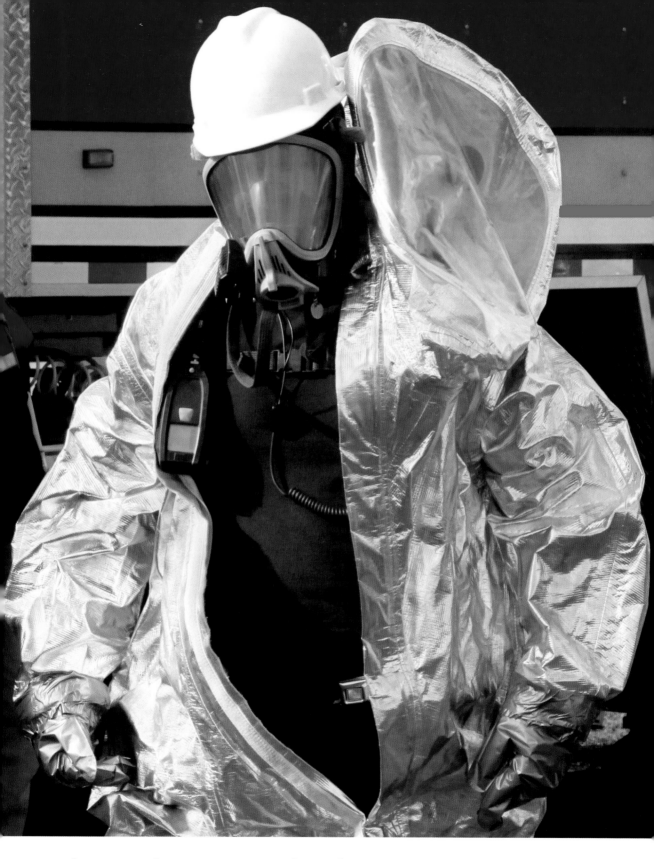

After using this equipment in a hazardous environment, hazmat workers will have to be decontaminated, or washed off, before they can remove the protective clothing.

Many hazmat vehicles are built with a communications or command center, typically with radios, video screens, digital cameras, and even fresh and gray water tanks.

Hazmat teams usually respond to emergencies in a truck that's similar to a small fire truck. The trucks are loaded with all the gear they need. They use hoses and vacuums to suck up liquids, chemicals to **neutralize** other chemicals, and absorbent material to soak up liquids. They also have a well-stocked supply of pumps, aprons, and gloves. The trucks may even carry a large portable shower unit. These showers are used spray off people who have been covered with a toxic substance.

So, You Want to Be on a Hazmat Team?

If you're interested in working on a hazmat team, you will probably want to train as a firefighter first. Chemicals can cause fires and explosions, so it is important to know firefighting techniques. To become a firefighter, you train at a fire academy where you learn how to put out fires and help people who have been hurt. After working as a firefighter, you can get additional training and take a special test to become certified as a hazmat team member.

To learn more look up:

http://www.hazmatfc.com/Pages/Home.aspx

After working with dangerous chemicals, a hazmat worker must decontaminate before unsuiting.

Hazmat teams don't just protect the community against accidents. They also respond to calls in which police suspect **terrorism**.

After the terrorist attacks of September 11, 2001, hazmat teams got lots of false calls. People were worried about terrorists launching **anthrax** attacks.

But some of these calls were not false. Several letters containing anthrax were sent to the post office, members of Congress, and different news outlets. Wearing containment suits, hazmat units were called to clean up the anthrax and preserve it for evidence. They helped anyone who had been exposed.

Hazmat members collect evidence from a potential crime scene during a drill.

Hazmat teams work together with fire departments, police, and city and state government. They make sure we are all kept safe from chemicals that can harm us and pollute our environment. Hazmat workers are smart, resourceful, quick-thinking, and brave. They're part of the large, strong network of emergency responders in our community.

During a mock terrorist attack, this hazmat worker collects samples of a white powder for further inspection.

TIMELINE

14th Century:
Doctors wear heavy suits and masks to try to protect themselves from bubonic plague.

1940s:
A version of the modern hazmat suit is first introduced.

1979:
A nuclear reactor partially melts down on Three Mile Island, New York. Large amounts of hazardous radiation are released, prompting mass evacuation.

1919:
Crystalized methamphetamine is first produced.

1977:
The first fire services hazardous materials team is formed in Jacksonville, Florida.

1994:
A cult in Japan releases nerve gas, killing nineteen people. Hazmat teams in the United States take notice.

2007:
The National Hazardous Materials Fusion Center, a group to help and support hazmat teams, is formed.

1986:
A train carrying toxic substances goes off the tracks near Miamisburg, Ohio. Hazmat teams respond.

2001:
Letters laced with anthrax are mailed to various locations around the U.S. in an act of domestic terrorism. Hazmat teams help contain the spread.

2008:
Three thousand people are evacuated near Lafayette, Louisiana after a train derailed, spilling toxic substances and prompting a large cleanup by hazmat teams.

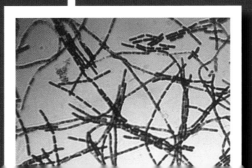

GLOSSARY

anthrax (AN-thraks): a disease that can be spread by airborne spores, usually fatal

deputies (DEP-yuh-tees): people appointed to act on behalf of others

evacuation (ih-vak-yoo-EY-shuhn): to leave an unsafe place

evaluate (ih-VAL-yoo-eyt): to look carefully at the nature of something or the qualities of something

hazardous (HAZ-er-duhs): dangerous

methamphetamine (meth-am-FET-uh-meen): a usually illegal drug made by mixing and cooking various substances

neutralize (NOO-truh-lahyz): to counteract something in order to make it ineffective

substances (SUHB-stuhns-iz): the physical state of something, what something is made of

terrorism (TER-uh-riz-uhm): the use of violence to achieve some purpose

INDEX

acid   11

anthrax   24

chemicals   4, 8, 10, 12, 14, 16, 17, 22, 23, 27

evacuate   15

fire department(s)   8, 10, 12, 15, 27

firefighters   8, 10, 12

hazardous material(s)   4, 6, 8

hazmat team(s)   4, 6, 8, 10, 11, 12, 15, 16, 20, 22, 23, 24, 27

meth lab(s)   16

terrorists   24

toxic   14, 22

SHOW WHAT YOU KNOW

1. What is one type of hazardous material?
2. What other job do many hazmat team members have?
3. When might a hazmat team need to organize an evacuation?
4. Name three things a hazmat team might bring when responding to an incident.
5. What did hazmat teams do to help during the anthrax scare of 2001?

WEBSITES TO VISIT

http://www.fortlauderdale.gov/fire-rescue/hazmat.htm

http://www.sccfd.org/clothing_hazmat.html

http://www.hazmatfc.com/Pages/Home.aspx

About the Author

Emma Carlson Berne has written over three dozen books for children and young adults on many different subjects. She lives in Cincinnati with her husband and two little boys. She is thankful that hazmat teams are well-trained and able to respond to any emergency.

Meet The Author!
www.meetREMauthors.com

www.rourkeeducationalmedia.com

PHOTO CREDITS: Cover courtesy U.S. Navy; page 4-5 © Ben Carlson; page 6-7 © Ben Carlson; page 8-9 © Dale A Stork, inset page 8 © Mark Winfrey; page 10 and 11 © TFoxFoto; page 12-13 © Ben Carlson, page 13 © Anton Oparin; page 14 map © Globe Turner, photo © Jerry Sharp, page 15 © worradirek; page 16 © wellphoto, page 17 Adam Gregor and TFoxFoto; page 18-19 courtesy of FEMA; page 20 courtesy U.S. Air Force, page 21 © Ben Carlson; page 22 © Bidgee, page 23 © TFoxFoto; page 24-25 courtesy of U.S. Marine Corps, Page 25 courtesy of FEMA; page 26-27 © U.S. Navy; page 28 © Globe Turner, page 29 © GEOATLAS - GRAPHI-OGRE (map) and Centers for Disease Control

Edited by: Jill Sherman

Designed and Produced by Nicola Stratford   www.nicolastratford.com

Library of Congress Cataloging-in-Publication Data

Carlson Berne. Emma
  Hazmat: Disposing Toxic Materials / Emma Carlson Berne
  p. cm. -- (Emergency Response)
  ISBN 978-1-62717-658-3 (hard cover) (alk. paper)
  ISBN 978-1-62717-780-1 (soft cover)
  ISBN 978-1-62717-899-0 (e-book)
 Library of Congress Control Number: 2014934251

Rourke Educational Media
Printed in the United States of America,
North Mankato, Minnesota

Also Available as:

ROURKE'S
e-Books